Contents

Hands off!

Pharaoh Pepi II used to cover some of his slaves in honey and watch the flies swarm – hilarious?

What pops into your head when you think of ancient Egypt? Mysterious mummies and stunning monuments? Fascinating pharaohs and great gods? Top marks if you thought of any of those. But how much do you really know about this ancient civilization? Did you know that ancient Egyptian mummies weren't called, er, mummies? Or that female pharaohs wore beards?

Can you believe that Pharaoh Pepi II got a buzz out of using some of his slaves as honey-coated flypaper? And that Tutankhamun married his half-sister? Ewwwww.

This book will transport you to the very heart of ancient Egypt to reveal fascinating facts about the ancient civilization that lasted for over 3,000 years.

Around 500 BCE, the ancient Greek Herodotus became one of the earliest travelers to visit ancient Egypt and write about it. The trouble was, Herodotus couldn't speak the language and sometimes got a little mixed up.

Nowadays it's mainly sailors and old ladies who have all the beardy fun. Not so in ancient Egypt...

AWFULLY ANCIENT

Mangy Mummies, Menacing Pharaohs, and the Awful Afterlife

A Moth–Eaten History of the Extraordinary Egyptians!

Kay Barnham

Gareth Stevens PUBLISHING

Please visit our website, **www.garethstevens.com**. For a free color catalog of all our high-quality books, call toll-free 1-800-542-2595 or fax 1-877-542-2596.

Library of Congress Cataloging-in-Publication Data

Barnham, Kay.
Mangy mummies, menacing pharaohs, and the awful afterlife: a moth-eaten history of the extraordinary Egyptians! / by Kay Barnham.
p. cm. — (Awfully ancient)
Includes index.
ISBN 978-1-4824-3125-4 (pbk.)
ISBN 978-1-4824-3128-5 (6 pack)
ISBN 978-1-4824-3126-1 (library binding)
1. Egypt — Civilization — To 332 B.C. — Juvenile literature.
2. Egypt — History — To 332 B.C. — Juvenile literature.
I. Barnham, Kay. II. Title.
DT61.B37 2016
932'.01 —d23

Published in 2016 by
Gareth Stevens Publishing
111 East 14th Street, Suite 349
New York, NY 10003

Copyright © 2016 Wayland / Gareth Stevens

Senior editor: Julia Adams
Illustrator: Tom Morgan-Jones
Designer: Rocket Design (East Anglia) Ltd.

Manufactured in the United States of America

CPSIA compliance information: Batch #CS15GS.
For further information contact Gareth Stevens, New York, New York at 1-800-542-2595.

Do you suffer from hair loss? If so, you might (not) want to check out some of our rub-in remedies on page 20.

Learn about the little ones, page 24

Wanna make a mummy? Turn to page 6 to learn the insides and outs.

Everything either side of the flooded area of the Nile is basically desert.

He may have gotten some things wrong, but Herodotus still provided some useful insights into ancient Egyptian life.

But he did get one thing absolutely right, and that was the importance of the River Nile. Long ago, the great river flooded the surrounding land every year and left behind a rich deposit of glorious mud, making the soil extremely fertile and the ideal place for people to live and to grow crops. "Egypt is the gift of the Nile," said Herodotus, because without it, Egypt as we know it simply wouldn't have existed.

A LOOK BACK IN TIME

The Nile is the longest river in the world, measuring a whopping 4,132 miles (6,650 km) from source to sea. It ends in the Mediterranean Sea. But where does this magnificent river actually begin? It was John Hanning Speke, a Victorian adventurer, who found out the answer over 150 years ago. He tracked the river's source down to Lake Victoria in central Africa. There are no prizes for guessing who he named the lake after.

Mangy Mummies

Long hooks were used to drag out the brains – ew!

Canopic jars like these were used to store all the scooped out sloppy body bits.

An ancient Egyptian who turned dead people into mummies was called an embalmer. They made sure that a body was so well preserved, it would stay in excellent condition for thousands of years.

Hold your nose

The embalmer's workshop wouldn't have been a very pleasant place to be. Just imagine lungs, livers, and long coils of intestines soaking in preserving salts, while flies buzz overhead before landing on blood–soaked sand, and you've sort of got the picture. Urgh.

All dried out

More than half of a person's body is made of water. So once the embalmers had dried it out, a mummy was not only stiff, but quite light, too.

Mummy-mummiya!

Egyptians didn't use the term "mummy" to describe a preserved, bandaged body! "Mummy" comes from the much more modern Arabic word "mummiya," meaning the wax or bitumen — black, squishy stuff — that was used to seal coffins. Archaeologists have found two words that the ancient Egyptians used to describe mummies: "khrts," which means "bodies," and "twts," meaning "images."

Inside-out

If the dead person's organs and other squishy bits were left inside the body, bacteria would grow and the whole mummy would go rotten. So the embalmer's first job was to take all the insides out.

The embalmer poked a long hook up the nose and dragged out the brain. Anything left behind was scraped out with a long-handled ladle. Next, the abdomen was cut open and all the organs removed — except one. The heart was left untouched, because the mummy was going to need it to travel to the afterlife. The intestines were hauled out and, along with the organs, washed in palm oil and stored in canopic jars, ready to pop in the tomb, too. Then the empty body was packed with salts and left to dry out for 40 to 70 days before being wrapped in bandages.

A LOOK BACK IN TIME

MIY (Mummify It Yourself)
Or
A Short Guide to Instant Mummification

Poor people couldn't afford the HUGE costs of mummification, so they buried their dead in the desert instead. The hot, dry sand did a pretty good job of soaking up the body fluids and within a couple of years the corpse became a perfect quick, cheap mummy anyway.

Ahh, this is the life – er, I mean death!

The Ba and the Ka

Charming!

Embalmers murmured sacred prayers as they mummified a body. They also tucked lucky charms between the bandages as they wrapped the mummy up.

The ancient Egyptians believed the human soul had five parts: the heart, the shadow, the name, and two spirits called the Ba and the Ka. It was because of these spirits that embalmers went to so much trouble to make the mummy look as good as possible.

Spiriting away

Ba was a person's character, and Ka their life force. While the person was alive, both spirits lived inside the body. Yet after death, the Ba was free to roam anywhere in the world as long as when night fell, it returned to the body. Meanwhile, the Ka had to remain in the tomb and needed food to survive, so relatives of the deceased left food at the tomb for the spirit to eat. But before the journey to the afterlife could begin, both the Ba and the Ka had to return to the mummified body. And the only way they could find their way back to the right body was if they recognized it.

Staying in the tomb and getting treats sounds like a pretty good deal to us...

Hmmmm, cookies.

Golden toes

After his death, each of the Pharaoh Tutankhamun's toes was placed in a gold sheath, marked with grooves that looked like nails and skin creases.

Makeup was applied on the bandages.

Shhhh!

Looks nothing like him!

Woah! I've heard of onions making your eyes water, but this is something else...

So it was important for the embalmers to make the mummy's face look as much like the person's face as possible — when they were still alive, of course. The skin of the dead body was massaged to make it supple. Padding was placed under the skin, so that it looked plump and healthy. Finally, the face was made up with eyeliner and rouge.

A LOOK BACK IN TIME

Mummification 101

Mummification was a long and difficult process. Things could — and did — go wrong. But embalmers were pretty good at putting things right again. Here are just some of the tricks of the trade.

Teeth falling out?

Not a problem! Just wire them back into the jaw.

Hand or toe dropping off?

Simply replace it with a wooden one.

Eye popping out?

Stuff an onion into the empty socket!

Head snapped off?

Jam it back into place with a sharp stick.

Nose collapses while removing the brain?

Just stuff two small rolls of papyrus (paper made from reeds) up the nostrils.

Destination: AFTERLIFE!

(and how to get there)

Babi, the giant baboon, is just one of the many gods who guards the afterlife.

Ever wondered how a mummy traveled to the afterlife? Then put yourself in their shoes, or, um, bandages, and prepare to find out just how fraught with danger the journey was supposed to be.

Your challenge is to make the dangerous journey through the Duat — the netherworld. It's also known as the land of the dead and exists between life on Earth and the afterlife, where you are guaranteed a life of loveliness. Are you ready?

1 The coffin is held upright and the priest performs the opening-of-the-mouth ceremony with a model of an adze – a stone ax. Ouch!

2 The jackal-headed god Anubis enters your tomb and wakes you for the journey ahead.

3 A dead man called Sennedjem stands at the gate to the other world.

4 Isis, a protective goddess with powerful spells, greets you and guides you to the Western Mountain and the Gate to the Netherworld.

5 Now battle your way past the snake- and knife-wielding god Apophis, before fighting Sobek, the crocodile-headed, lion-chested, hippo-rumped Devourer.

6 You are now descending the river to the Gallery of the Night. This is the gloomy realm of the god Seth (god of the desert, storms, disorder and violence).

7 Can you fight off the giant baboon, Babi, who attempts to overturn your boat? He is very bloodthirsty and lives off the entrails of animals he kills. (Urgh.)

8 Now climb up the Staircase of Justice. Remember to bow to the Ka gods of creation as you go.

9 Finally, you must face the weighing-of-the-heart ceremony, conducted by Anubis. To enter the afterlife, your heart must weigh less than a feather.

Are you heavy-hearted?

Oh dear. You've done too many bad things during your lifetime, which means that you will be devoured by the demon crocodile-headed god Ammut and will be lost forever. You've failed to reach the afterlife. Sorry about that.

YOU LOSE!

Are you light-hearted?

Hooray! Prepare to enter a world where dancers and musicians will greet you, where there's always enough food and where you will remain in good health forever. Welcome to the afterlife!

YOU WIN!

Ye Gods and Goddesses!

Osiris was a really nice god. He taught people about farming and stuff.

The ancient Egyptians believed that their gods had feelings, just like ordinary people. There were an awful lot of gods — over 2,000 of them — and the most important of these were Osiris, Isis, and Set. But they didn't exactly get on...

The evil plot

At the beginning of time, it's said that Osiris taught people how to farm and was loved by everyone. Everyone, that is, except his jealous brother Set. His mind dark with hatred, Set plotted to kill his brother. He lured him to a feast, locked him inside a chest and threw this into the Nile. But Set had not reckoned with Isis, the brave sister and wife of Osiris. She tracked him down and helped him to return to Egypt. Foolishly, Osiris forgave his brother. Set fumed. He'd now been humiliated.

Murder!

Set plotted to do away with his brother for good by murdering him. He would hack the body into pieces. Because if there was no body, then he couldn't be blamed for the murder. He carried out his plan and threw the pieces of Osiris into the Nile.

Isis to the rescue

But Isis had magical powers and tracked down all the pieces of Osiris' body. She called upon the god named Anubis for help and together they wrapped the broken body in bandages to create the very first mummy! Anubis leaned over the corpse and breathed life back into Osiris' body.

Revenge

Unknown to Set, however, Isis and Osiris had a son named Horus, who had been hidden away from his evil uncle. Horus attacked Set, who whipped up blinding sandstorms to confuse him. Set tore an eye from Horus but, after a furious struggle, Horus defeated him. There was no forgiveness this time. Set was banished to the underworld.

THE END

Fabulous Pharaohs

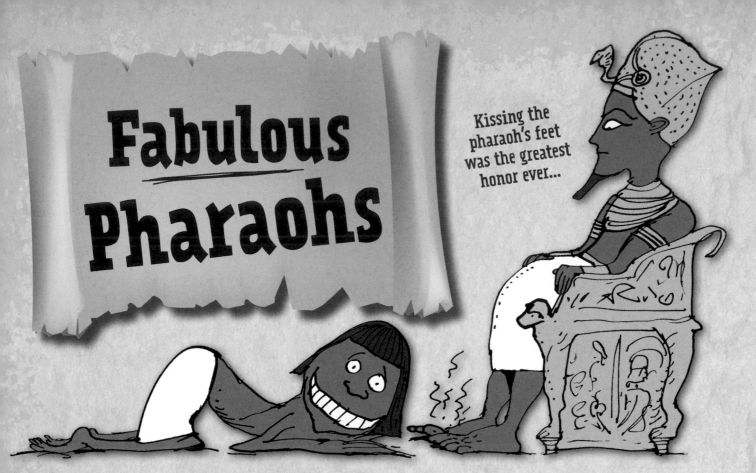

Kissing the pharaoh's feet was the greatest honor ever...

According to the ancient Egyptians, Ra the sun god ruled the skies and Osiris ruled the afterlife. But in Egypt itself, it was the pharaoh who was most definitely in charge. And their power was awesome.

A day in the life of a pharaoh

This was not as relaxing as you might expect. Every day, a pharaoh had to offer food to their ancestors' spirits and take part in endless religious ceremonies. When they ate, there were strict routines, because the meal was said to be an offering to a god. In fact, the word "pharoah" actually means "great house," because their body was believed to be the home of the god Horus. They also spent time examining reports and dishing out instructions to educated officials, called scribes.

...but touching the pharoah's scepter, even by accident, carried the death penalty.

And don't come back!

A LOOK BACK IN TIME
Two top pharaohs

Hatshepsut wore a fake beard to show she was in charge.

Ramesses II
(1279–1213 BCE)

Also known as Ramesses the Great, this pharaoh is said to be one of the most fabulous ever. He led his armies to victory on the northern and southern borders of Egypt, as well as clearing the coasts of pirates. Meanwhile, he had a lot of wives (possibly eight) and a huge number of children (well over a hundred). Naturally, he had a massive tomb too. It's not surprising that he earned the title "Great."

Hatshepsut
(1473–1458 BCE)

Hatshepsut was first a queen, reigning with her husband, the pharaoh Thutmose II. But when he died, she didn't want to give up the throne to her nephew Thutmose III. So Hatshepsut became pharaoh herself. Her reign was very successful. She built obelisks and grand temples and the Egyptian economy boomed. Sadly, after she died, many references to Hatshepsut vanished, possibly erased by her nephew who had gotten the throne at last.

Who Killed Tutankhamun?

Tutankhamun (reigned 1333–23 BCE) is perhaps the most famous pharaoh of them all. But this isn't because of anything he did during his short lifetime. He didn't become a proper celebrity until after his tomb was discovered in 1922. When archaeologists unwrapped his mummy, they noticed a dark patch of dried blood on the back of Tutankhamun's skull. Wow. Did this mean he was murdered?!

The facts

Tutankhamun became pharaoh in 1333 BCE when he was just nine. Because he was so young, he had advisors — General Horemheb and Ay, the vizier or prime minster — who helped him to rule the country.

After Tutankhamun died aged 19, Ankhesenamun — his widow and half-sister — wanted to marry a prince from a nearby kingdom, but the prince mysteriously died on the way to Egypt. And soon after that, Ankhesenamun married Ay, her grandfather. He became the new

Can't wait to show my friends this awesome throne!

Ancient Egyptians thought nothing of marrying their grandparents – eww!

Tip-top tomb!

Ever since ancient Egyptian times, robbers had a nasty habit of ransacking tombs. But Tutankhamun's tomb was in almost perfect condition when it was discovered in 1922. Archaeologists were delighted!

pharaoh, but not for long, because Horemheb overthrew Ay. Now he was the new pharaoh instead!

So was Tutankhamun finished off by someone who wanted to be pharaoh or was there another reason? Why *did* he die?

The theories

• He was assassinated by Ay, the pharaoh who came to power after Tutankhamun.

This definitely seems like an unpleasant scenario...

• He was murdered by Horemheb, the army general.

• He died because of a broken leg that had become infected.

• It was because of genetic defects, caused because his parents were closely related.

Other theories include that he may have been skewered by a hippopotamus or simply died from malaria.

The truth...?

When his body was first discovered, some suspected that Tutankhamun had been murdered. But now most believe that he'd had an accident. And because he was already in poor health due to genetic conditions inherited from his parents (who were either siblings or cousins), this may have speeded up his death.

A Who's Who of Ancient Egypt

Viziers took care of collecting taxes and running the country.

Not everyone could be a pharaoh, of course. So what about the rest of the ancient Egyptians? What did they do for a living?

Viziers

These government officials were the pharaoh's top people. They helped to run the country, by giving the pharaoh advice and carrying out his orders. Pharaohs chose the viziers themselves, often from their own families.

Priests and nobles

These jobs were only open to the super rich. Priests spent their days performing rituals, such as offering the statues of the gods clothes, jewels, and food. Meanwhile, nobles served the pharaoh by looking after their treasure or preparing the royal tomb for burial.

Scribes

There were only a lucky few ancient Egyptians who could read and write. These were the scribes, and they kept records of EVERYTHING. It was a good job they did, too. It's because of the scribes that we know so much about life in ancient Egypt today.

Craftsmen

Egypt had a small but important group of artists and craftsmen. Some made pottery, shoes, and clothes, while the more skilled would make beautiful objects for the rich.

Peasants

And finally, there were the peasants. They were the farmers, the unskilled laborers, and the construction workers, who built the pyramids and tombs.

Pharaoh

Viziers

Priests

Scribes

Craftsmen

Farmers

Slaves

The great ancient Egyptian pyramid!

Ancient Egyptian society was shaped a lot like a pyramid. On the top, there was a single pharaoh. Then beneath were a few viziers, then a larger number of priests and nobles, and so on. At the very bottom of the pyramid were the slaves, laborers, and peasants; there were more of these than any other social group.

What's up, Doc?

Better?

In ancient Egypt, you couldn't just reach for a pair of glasses, you had pigs' eyes poured in your ears!

Pardon?

It wasn't surprising that, in a hot, dusty climate, nasty diseases and infections were everywhere. Ancient Egyptians had remedies to fix them. However, some were mad, some were bad and some were positively dangerous. Here are just a few...

Going bald?

Mix together ox fat, lion fat, hippo fat, goose fat, snake fat, cat fat, crocodile fat, ibex fat, and serpent fat. Rub the mixture onto a bald head.

Poor eyesight?

Grind up a pig's eye. Add honey and red ochre (this made the mixture turn red). Then pour the mixture into your patient's ear.

Stinking cold?

Drink the milk from a mother who's just had a baby boy. Then say a magic spell. (Though, to be fair, this would have been about as effective as any other cold remedy that's ever been invented.)

Unsurprisingly, there are no reports of all this fat actually helping grow hair back...

Top docs

Even though these remedies might sound a bit silly, it didn't mean that the ancient Egyptians were no good at being doctors. They actually knew an awful lot about the human body and how it worked. They knew all about breathing, the pulse, the brain, and the liver, and they knew how the nose worked, too. Ancient Egyptian doctors were aware of the link between the pulse and the heart, but not of the way blood circulates around the body.

When it came to cuts or broken bones, ancient Egyptian doctors were experts. They cleaned wounds, stitched them, and used bandages. And they were pretty good at treating fractures with splints, too. In fact, ancient Egyptian doctors were so highly respected that many foreign kings asked for their help.

Stinking cold?

This seems like an exceptionally bad idea...

You want what?!

A LOOK BACK IN TIME

From doctor to god

Imhotep (c.2650–2600 BCE) wasn't just a doctor. Here's his full title: Chancellor of the King of Egypt, Doctor, First in line after the Upper King of Upper Egypt, Administrator of the Great Palace, Hereditary nobleman, High Priest of Heliopolis, Builder, Chief Carpenter, Chief Sculptor, and Maker of Vases in Chief. Phew! His medical and many other achievements were regarded so highly that, 2,000 years after he died, Imhotep was made a god of medicine and healing.

Puzzling Pyramids

A piece of cake

The ancient Egyptians didn't call them pyramids. The English word "pyramid" comes from the Greek word "pyramis." This was a type of wheat cake that was baked in the shape of a pyramid.

For many, pyramids symbolize ancient Egypt. They are structures made from blocks of stone. Archaeologists love them, because they have helped us to find out even more about the ancient Egyptians...

What's inside?

Since ancient Egyptian times, many have wondered what pyramids actually are. Guesses have included: stone computers, observatories and even alien landing sites. But pyramids are, of course, none of these things.

These ancient superstructures are actually grand tombs, with enough room inside for the mummified body of the dead pharaoh — or other very important person — and everything they needed for their journey to the afterlife, too. And that means EVERYTHING.

Some pyramids even included a toilet. And pharaohs didn't want to be lonely on their journey to the afterlife, so they took mummified pets with them. Models of their servants went into the pyramid, too.

A LOOK BACK IN TIME

Shifting the load

The Great Pyramid at Giza was built as a burial place for the Pharaoh Khufu (2589–2566 BCE). Over two million blocks of limestone were used in its construction, which may have taken as long as 20 years. But how did the workers move the huge stone blocks? Scientists think that they now know: workers simply poured water onto the sand and – tadaaaa! – the stones were MUCH easier to drag.

Tomb raiders

Unfortunately, pyramids were hugely tempting to thieves. They were easy to spot and guaranteed to be filled with riches. This is why later pharaohs were buried in tombs – they were much easier to hide.

Buried alive

In very early tombs, a few pharaohs were buried with their actual servants. Yikes.

Young Egyptians

Egyptian kids had lots of fun things to play with. They were mostly made of wood and leather.

If you reached childhood in ancient Egypt, you were doing well, because nearly a third of babies died before their first birthday. Infection and disease were usually to blame.

Do you feel lucky?

However, as far as the ancient Egyptians were concerned, infection and disease had nothing to do with it. A person's future was settled as soon as they were born by Seshat, goddess of wisdom, knowledge and writing. (Oh, and architecture, astronomy, astrology, building, mathematics, and surveying, too. She was VERY intelligent.) Seshat was said to predict exactly how long everyone would live.

The poor little Egyptians who didn't make it were put in clay vessels that were placed under the floor of the house to bring good luck.

Wooden horse

A LOOK BACK IN TIME

What's in a name?

If names are anything to go by, then ancient Egyptians simply adored their children. Just look at what they called them!

Boys' names	Girls' names
Adofo – fighter	Azizi – precious
Baabfemi – beloved of his father	Femi – love
Bomani – warrior	Mandesi – sweet
Hasani – handsome	Nefret – pretty

Sometimes, parents added the name of a top god or goddess to their child's name to give them protection. And let's face it, they needed it.

If they hadn't lived long, babies were left at the edge of the desert or thrown into the Nile.

A short childhood

If ancient Egyptians were lucky enough to reach childhood, it looks as if it was fun. Tomb paintings show them cradling pets. Meanwhile, archaeologists have found all sorts of toys, including rag dolls, model animals, and wooden or leather balls. Even better, children weren't nagged to hurry up and get dressed, because they ran around naked until the age of nine or ten. And they didn't have to brush their hair, either, because heads were usually shaved, leaving just a small plait over the right ear.

Girls usually didn't go to school, but learned how to do housework instead, while sons of craftsmen learned their fathers' trades. Boys from wealthy families were trained to be scribes, priests and army officers.

But around the time kids became teenagers, the fun was over. Because this was when Egyptians married and had children themselves.

← An ancient rag doll

Let's Party!

twang!

pling!

The ancient Egyptians celebrated the days dedicated to their gods and goddesses. They celebrated the anniversaries of great victories. And they celebrated the anniversaries of their pharaohs' coronations, too. This meant that there were a LOT of parties. Some lasted just one day; others lasted for many. There were processions, ceremonies, chants and speeches. And food. Lots of food.

Looking good...

Ancient Egyptians wanted to look their very best at parties. Both men and women wore eye makeup to make them look just like the god Horus. Their eyes were rimmed with a black eyeliner called kohl, which was made from lead. They wore green eye paint made from a mineral called malachite.

Meanwhile, they wore red ochre – reddish clay that was mined and left out to dry – on their cheeks and palms. Finally, they colored their hair and nails using a dye made from the henna plant.

...smelling great!

When they arrived at a party, guests were welcomed with garlands of fragrant flowers. But the climate was so hot that partygoers wanted to make sure they smelled lovely all through the party. So they each wore a wax cone on their head which, as it melted through their wigs, gave off beautifully scented perfumes. Mmmm.

That's a coincidence!

In ancient Egyptian times, December 25 was the day everyone celebrated the birth of the god Horus.

Not quite like the deodorant we use nowadays...

It's party time!

Can I borrow your kohl again, Tracey?

Sure thing, Jeff. We'll have to give the kids makeup lessons soon too, you know...

Time to dance!

No ancient Egyptian party would have been complete without music and dancing. Musicians played harps, lyres, lutes, and percussion instruments, while acrobats and dancers entertained the guests.

A LOOK BACK IN TIME

Food, glorious food

At parties, ancient Egyptians feasted on grains, fruit, vegetables and fish. Grapes, pomegranates, and melons were on the menu because they thrived in a hot, arid climate. Dates were a sweet treat. Meat was more expensive because grazing land was scarce, so only the rich dined on beef.

The poor had to make do with unleavened bread, onions and beer to drink. In times of famine, there are records of the poor even eating papyrus – a plant used to make a type of paper.

27

THE END

A bath's too wet without one!

There were many reasons why the ancient Egyptian civilization came to an end. There were civil wars. The Egyptian weapons weren't very sturdy. Another reason was that ancient Egypt was a victim of its own success. It was a country so rich and so fabulous that other countries were jealous. They wanted ancient Egypt for themselves. And the best way to take over another country was to invade it.

Myth vs Fact

It's said that Cleopatra committed suicide by letting a venomous type of cobra bite her, but this is just a myth. The fabulous Egyptian pharaoh probably took a lethal dose of poison.

Cleopatra is also said to have bathed in the milk of 700 asses every single day. This might actually be true, though. And the lactic acid in milk is supposed to make skin look lovely and healthy. So perhaps this is why she was so beautiful.

The mighty Persians

The Persian Empire, one of Egypt's powerful neighbors, attacked in 525 BCE and the country fell easily. The Persians were in charge for over a century. But then the ancient Egyptians fought back and the country was theirs from 404 to 342 BCE, when the Persians won again. However, the Persians weren't winners for long...

The Greek takeover

When Alexander the Great (356–323 BCE) arrived in Egypt in 332 BCE, he wasn't sightseeing like the many Greeks before him. He'd come to conquer the country! And after he'd beaten the ancient Egyptians, he went on to destroy the Persian Empire, too. When

Alexander died, the new ruler was Ptolemy I from Greece. The Greeks supported the ancient Egyptian culture, but Greek influences were everywhere. And the new official language was, of course, Greek as well.

The last pharaoh

Cleopatra VII, who ruled Egypt from 51–30 BCE, was a descendant of Ptolemy I. She was famous for her beauty and her men — top Romans Julius Caesar and Mark Antony. But she couldn't beat the Roman Empire. Cleopatra was the last Egyptian pharaoh.

It was all over for the ancient Egyptians.

Glossary

Ammut: crocodile-headed god

Anubis: jackal-headed god

Arsinoe: Cleopatra's sister

Ay: Tutankhamun's advisor

Babi: baboon god

canopic jars: jars in which the organs of the dead were placed

Cleopatra: the last pharaoh of Egypt

Duat: the netherworld between Earth and the afterlife

embalmer: prepared the mummies for burial

Hatshepsut: famous female pharaoh

Herodotus: a Greek traveler in ancient Egypt

Horemheb: Tutankhamun's general

Isis: wife of Osiris

Ka and Ba: twin spirits in every human

kohl: black eyeliner

mummies: embalmed bodies of the dead

natron: the salt in which the bodies of the dead were preserved

Osiris: chief god

papyrus: a type of paper made from reeds

pharaoh: god-king ruler of Egypt

Ptolemy: first Greek pharaoh

pyramids: ancient tombs of the early pharaohs

Ra: the sun god

Ramesses II: a powerful pharaoh who conquered an Empire

scribe: writer and recorder

Set: god of the underworld

Tutankhamun: the pharaoh whose tomb was found undisturbed

Vizier: advisor to the pharaoh

That just about wraps it up, folks!

More information

Places to visit

Field Museum, Chicago, Illinois
You can explore Inside Ancient Egypt, an exhibition that has two authentic rooms from a 5,000-year-old tomb. The Field Museum has one of the largest collections of mummies in the U.S.
http://www.fieldmuseum.org/at-the-field/exhibitions/inside-ancient-egypt

British Museum, London, UK
This museum has many permanent displays of ancient Egyptian artifacts and even mummies!
www.britishmuseum.org

National Museum of Scotland, Edinburgh, UK
Discover what ancient Egyptian coffins looked like, as well as jewelry and grooming equipment!
www.nms.ac.uk/our_museums/national_museum.aspx

Egyptian Centre, Swansea University, Swansea, UK
Discover an amazing 5,000-strong collection of artifacts, including canopic jars and amulets.
http://www.egypt.swan.ac.uk

Websites

http://www.historyforkids.net/ancient-egypt.html
Learn all about ancient Egyptian life, from how they built the pyramids to how they maintained crops in the desert.

http://www.watchknowlearn.org/Category.aspx?CategoryID=737
Check out this collection of videos that explain ancient Egypt!

www.childrensuniversity.manchester.ac.uk/interactives/history/egypt/
A great site from the Children's University of Manchester. Learn how to write in hieroglyphs!

Publisher's note to educators and parents: Our editors have carefully reviewed these websites to ensure that they are suitable for students. Many websites change frequently, however, and we cannot guarantee that a site's future contents will continue to meet our high standards of quality and educational value. Be advised that students should be closely supervised whenever they access the Internet.

Books

Truth or Busted: Female Pharaohs Wore False Beards! – The Fact or Fiction Behind the Egyptians by Kay Barnham, Wayland (2014)

The Gruesome Truth About the Egyptians by Jillian Powell, Wayland (2010)

Index